DOREEN VIRTUE, PH.D.

with Kristina Tracy

THANK YOU, ANGELS!

HAY HOUSE, INC.
Carlsbad, California • London
Sydney • Johannesburg • Vancouver
Hong Kong • New Delhi

Illustrated by Patricia Keeler

Published and distributed in the United States by: Hay House, Inc.: www.hayhouse.com • **Published and distributed in Australia by:** Hay House Australia Pty. Ltd.: www.hayhouse.com.au • **Published and distributed in the United Kingdom by:** Hay House UK, Ltd.: www.hayhouse.co.uk • **Published and distributed in the Republic of South Africa by:** Hay House SA (Pty), Ltd.: orders@ psdprom.co.za • www.hayhouse.co.za • **Distributed in Canada by:** Raincoast: www.raincoast.com • **Published in India by:** Hay House Publishers India: www.hayhouse.co.in

Design and editorial assistance: Jenny Richards • *Illustrations:* Patricia Keeler

Library of Congress Control Number: 2007928516

ISBN: 978-1-4019-1846-0

10 09 08 07   4 3 2 1
1st edition, October 2007

Printed in China

NOTE FROM DOREEN

Every kid and adult has guardian angels with them at all times. You've got angels with YOU right now! I wrote this book to help you learn about your angels and how to contact them. If you ever feel lonely or afraid, your angels can help you. If you need to find your homework or remember the answers to a test, your angels can help you. If you have a fight with your best friend or someone hurts your feelings, your angels can help you.

In fact, your angels can help you with EVERYTHING! The thing is, though, your angels can only help you if you ask them for help. That's because God gave everyone this thing called Free will, which means we have the right to make our own choices. The angels hope that you'll ask them for help a lot, because they love you and want you to be happy, healthy, and safe.

Remember: Whenever you need help of any kind . . . ask your angels!

Have you ever wondered what angels do all day?

Do we hang out in the sky
singing heavenly songs?

Are we relaxing on fluffy clouds?

Or playing the harp?

Do we watch over you from above?

Of course we do these kinds of things sometimes! We are angels, after all. But mostly we spend our time looking out for kids like you. Our work takes us all over the world, but we can be by your side in the blink of an eye. You might even be surprised by some of the jobs we take on.

Count on us to be there if you're feeling scared or worried. We won't fall asleep on the job!

We can also give you courage when you're trying something new or daring.

But wait . . . we're getting ahead of ourselves! First, there are a few things you should know about how we work.

One important thing you should know is that angels can't get started until you or someone who loves you asks! That's right! Angels aren't pushy. We wait patiently for you to call upon us.

To get in touch with us is easy. Just say
or think something like, "Angels . . .
please help me." We can hear you
no matter how you call us.

A "Dear Angels" note is a great way to tell us what you need. We may not have a mailbox, but we get the message loud and clear!

Pay attention, it could very well be an angel.
You'll be glad you did!

Angels also send you signs to let you know that they're near. Not like street signs, of course—theirs are much prettier. Look up—you might see an angel-shaped cloud or a colorful rainbow. Look down—that white feather is just for you!

Now that you know how we work, you're probably wondering, *How can an angel help me?* Angels help you every day in all kinds of ways!

For instance, if you have a date with the dentist and you're feeling worried, call on us!

We'll be with you the whole way. We'll calm your fears and help you know that everything will be all right— at the dentist's office or anywhere.

We also help you stay safe—we're your heavenly superheroes! We can save you from a speeding bus, leap between you and danger, and surround you with our protective light. It's a bird, it's a plane . . . it's an angel!

Angels have special healing powers, too. When you or someone you know is sick, call us! By the way . . . we can also be there for any of your animal friends!

Do you forget lots of stuff? Don't worry, everyone does—everyone except angels, that is. So if you are someone who forgets your helmet, your lunch money, or the words you studied for a test, just ask us! We're glad to be there with a friendly reminder when you need it most.

As you can see, angels keep busy! And when we want human help, we may send a person in our place—someone whose job it is to help you. You might recognize them:

doctors, nurses, lifeguards . . .

park rangers, police officers . . .

firefighters, paramedics,
rescue workers.

The most important thing to remember is that we love our job—
we love being there for you. When we look back on the day
we've shared, we feel great! And what do we ask in return,
you wonder? Not much really. Just a simple "Thank you."

"Thank you, angels!"

More about Angels . . .

Pay close attention to your thoughts and feelings—this is your intuition and an important way that angels speak to you.

Archangels are the leaders of the angels. They each have a special purpose. Call them by name when you need them.

Someone else can call on an angel for you. Or you can call on an angel for a person you care about.

Archangel Raphael is in charge of healing. This is the angel to call if you are sick or hurt.

No problem is too big or too small for an angel!

Everyone has a guardian angel.
Your guardian angel is with you
from the time you are born
and will always be
with you.

Archangel Michael is the
strongest and most powerful
angel. Call on him to help
and protect you anytime!

Spend some quiet time
each day listening
for your angels.

Archangel Raguel can help
you with problems with
friends, family,
teachers, and others.

Angels are never too busy for
you—they can actually help
many people at one time!

We hope you enjoyed this Hay House book. If you'd like to receive a free catalog featuring additional Hay House books and products, or if you'd like information about the Hay Foundation, please contact:

Hay House, Inc.
P.O. Box 5100
Carlsbad, CA 92018-5100

(760) 431-7695 or (800) 654-5126
(760) 431-6948 (fax) or (800) 650-5115 (fax)
www.hayhouse.com® • www.hayfoundation.org

PUBLISHED AND DISTRIBUTED IN AUSTRALIA BY: Hay House Australia Pty. Ltd., 18/36 Ralph St., Alexandria NSW 2015
Phone: 612-9669-4299 • Fax: 612-9669-4144 • www.hayhouse.com.au

PUBLISHED AND DISTRIBUTED IN THE UNITED KINGDOM BY: Hay House UK, Ltd., 292B Kensal Rd., London W10 5BE
Phone: 44-20-8962-1230 • Fax: 44-20-8962-1239 • www.hayhouse.co.uk

PUBLISHED AND DISTRIBUTED IN THE REPUBLIC OF SOUTH AFRICA BY: Hay House SA (Pty), Ltd., P.O. Box 990, Witkoppen 2068
Phone/Fax: 27-11-467-8904 • orders@psdprom.co.za • www.hayhouse.co.za

PUBLISHED IN INDIA BY: Hay House Publishers India, Muskaan Complex, Plot No. 3, B-2, Vasant Kunj, New Delhi 110 070
Phone: 91-11-4176-1620 • Fax: 91-11-4176-1630 • www.hayhouse.co.in

DISTRIBUTED IN CANADA BY: Raincoast, 9050 Shaughnessy St., Vancouver, B.C. V6P 6E5
Phone: (604) 323-7100 • Fax: (604) 323-2600 • www.raincoast.com

Tune in to HayHouseRadio.com® for the best in inspirational talk radio featuring top Hay House authors! And, sign up via the Hay House USA website to receive the Hay House online newsletter and stay informed about what's going on with your favorite authors. You'll receive bimonthly announcements about Discounts and Offers, Special Events, Product Highlights, Free Excerpts, Giveaways, and more!
www.HAYHOUSE.COM®